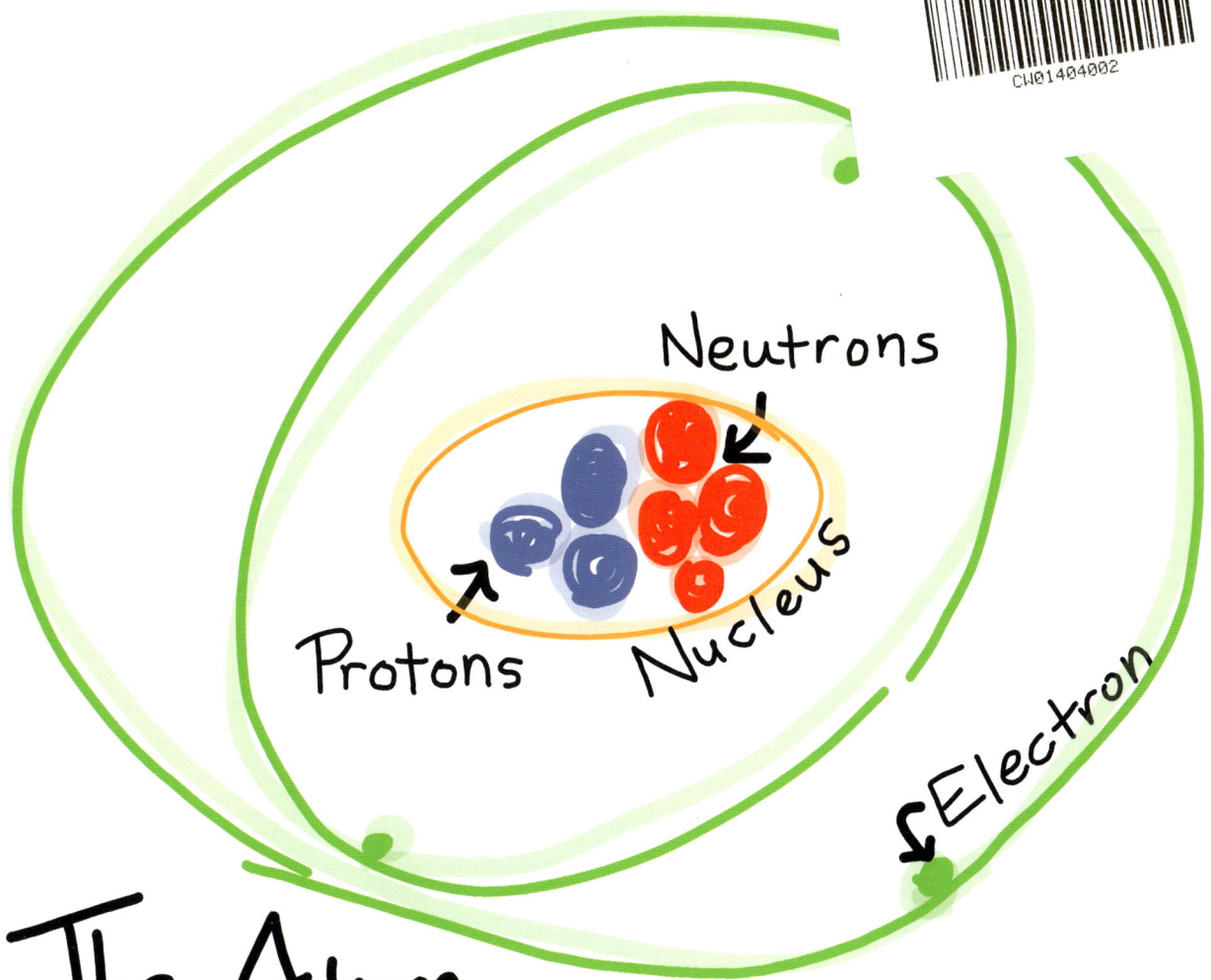

Neutrons

Nucleus

Protons

Electron

The Atom

Chemistry: the Atom and Elements

Written and Illustrated by: APRIL CHLOE TERRAZAS

dedicated to:

DR. IVERSON

OChem Professor Extraordinaire!!!

Thank you for making science FUN & exciting!

Chemistry: The Atom and Elements. April Chloe Terrazas, BS University of Texas at Austin.
Copyright © 2013 Crazy Brainz, LLC

Visit us on the web! www.Crazy-Brainz.com

Cover design, illustrations and text by: April Chloe Terrazas

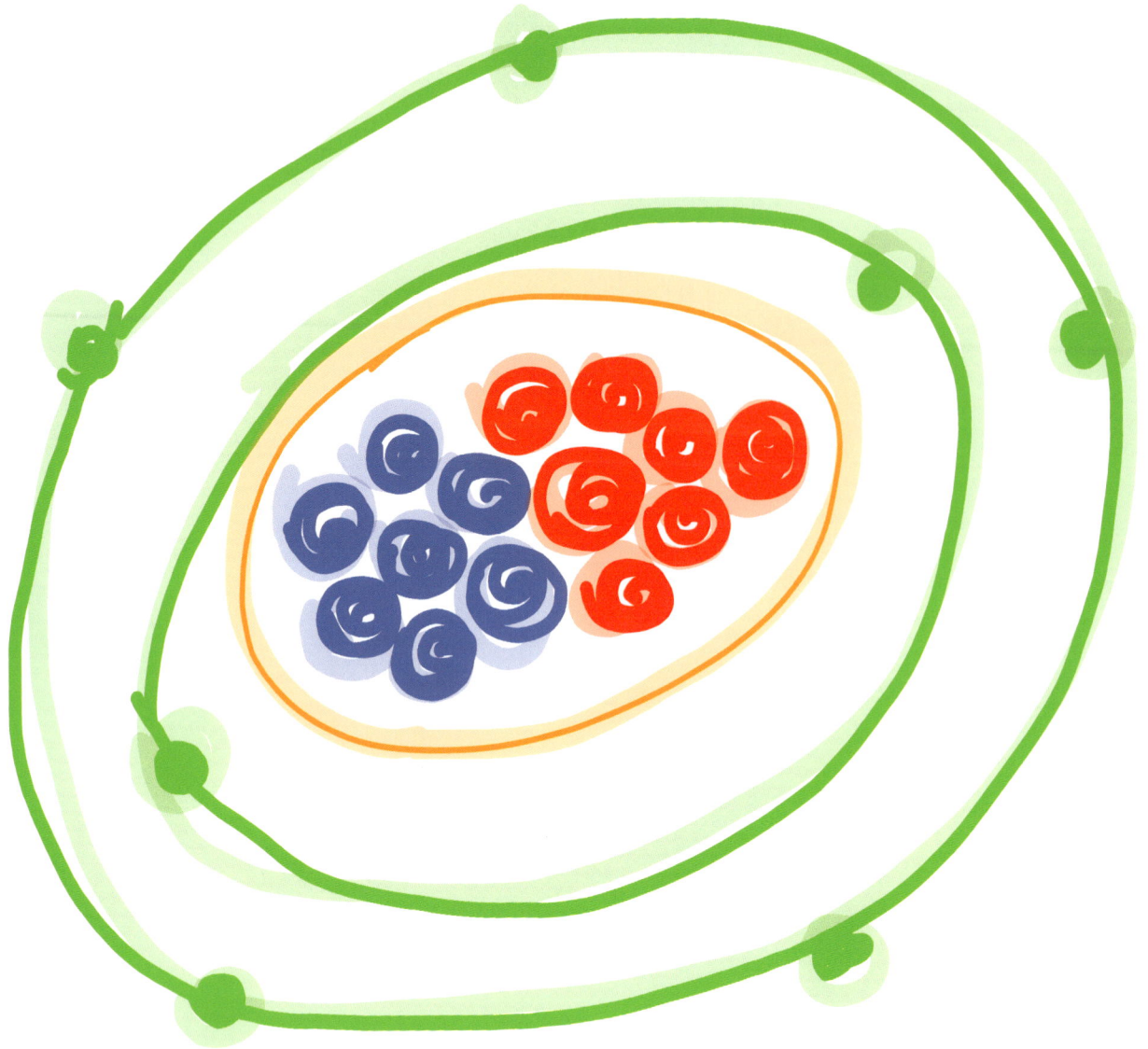

A-tom

El-e-ment

Sound it Out

1. A
2. TUM

Sound it Out

1. L
2. EH
3. MENT

This is an atom
of the element N.

Atoms contain
three different things.

Do you see the blue dots?
The red dots?
And the green dots?

The following pages will
teach you about atoms
and elements.

You are becoming a
Chemistry expert!

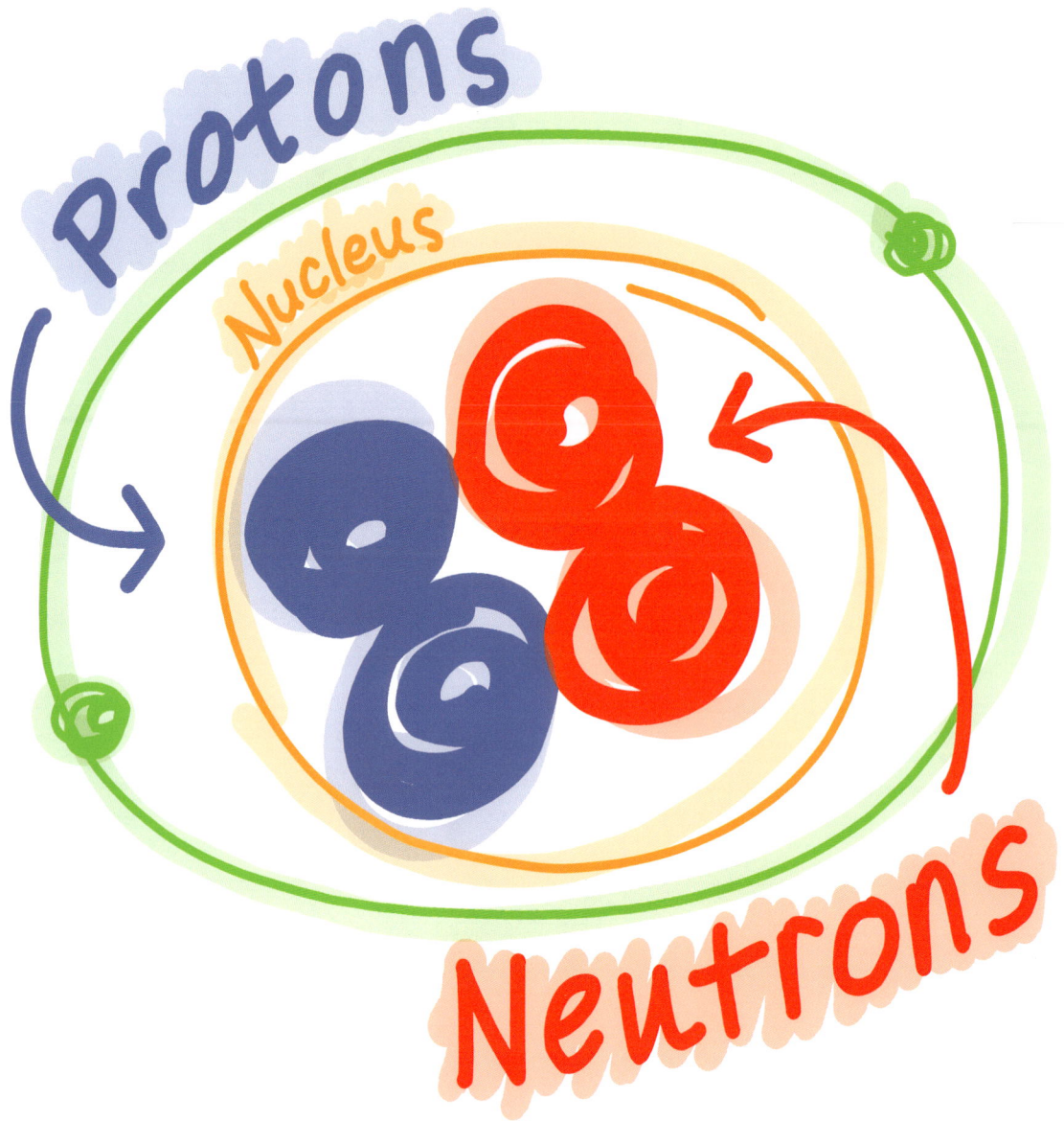

Pro-ton

Neu-tron

Nu-cle-us

Protons and neutrons are in the center of the atom.

The center of the atom is called the nucleus.

Different elements have different numbers of protons and neutrons in the nucleus.

What are the green dots around the nucleus?

Turn the page to find out!

Electrons

E-lec-tron

Electrons are outside the nucleus of the atom.

Do you see the electrons outside the nucleus of the atom?

Different elements have different numbers of electrons.

How many electrons are in this atom?

How many protons and neutrons are in this atom?

Periodic Table

1 H	
3 Li	4 Be
11 Na	12 Mg

Per-i-od-ic Ta-ble

This is the Periodic Table of Elements.

Inside each box is an element.

Of Elements

					2 He
5 B	6 C	7 N	8 O	9 F	10 Ne
13 Al	14 Si	15 P	16 S	17 Cl	18 Ar

Do you see the <u>number</u> next to each element?

This <u>number</u> is called the <u>atomic number</u>.

The <u>atomic number</u> tells you how many protons are inside the nucleus of an atom.

Periodic Table

1 **H**	
3 **Li**	4 **Be**
11 **Na**	12 **Mg**

Look at the element C, atomic number 6.

The 6 means that there are 6 **protons** inside the **nucleus** of an **atom** of the **element** C.

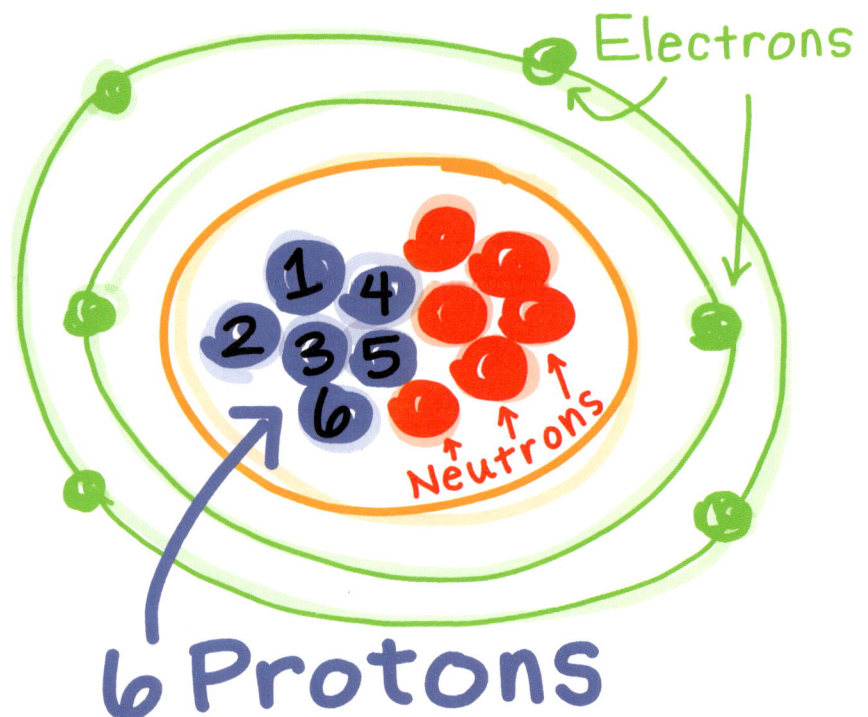

6
C

Electrons

1 2 3 4 5 6

Neutrons

6 Protons

Of Elements

					2 He
5 B	6 C	7 N	8 O	9 F	10 Ne
13 Al	14 Si	15 P	16 S	17 Cl	18 Ar

How many protons are inside the nucleus of an atom of the element Mg?

How many protons are inside the nucleus of an atom of the element Ar?

Are YOU ready

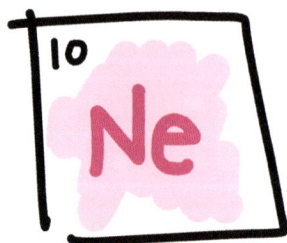

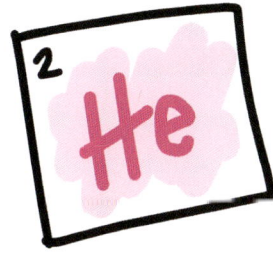

to learn
about
elements

???

³ Li

Lithium

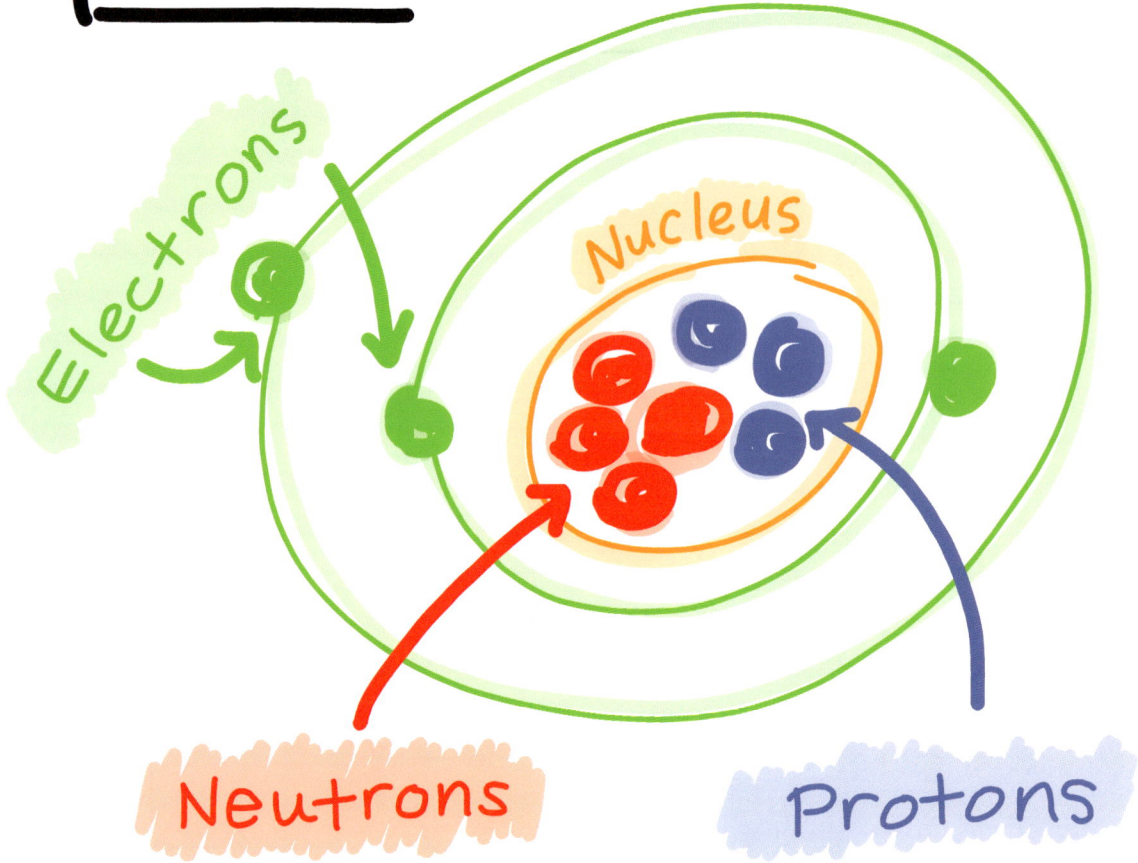

Electrons

Nucleus

Neutrons

Protons

Lith-i-um

Sound it Out

1. **LITH**
2. **EE**
3. **UM**

This is an atom of Lithium.
The symbol for Lithium is Li.

Did you see Li in the
Periodic Table of Elements?

What is the atomic number
of Lithium?

Lithium is in
medicine
and
batteries.

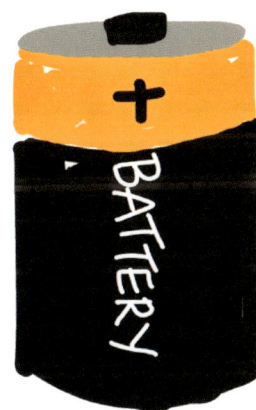

How many protons
are inside the nucleus
of an atom of Lithium?

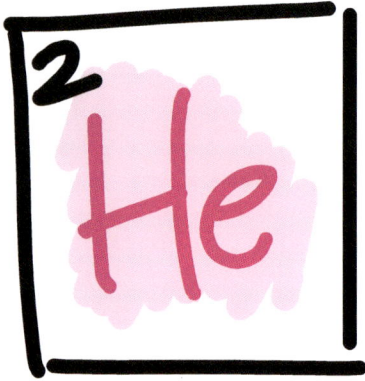

²He Helium

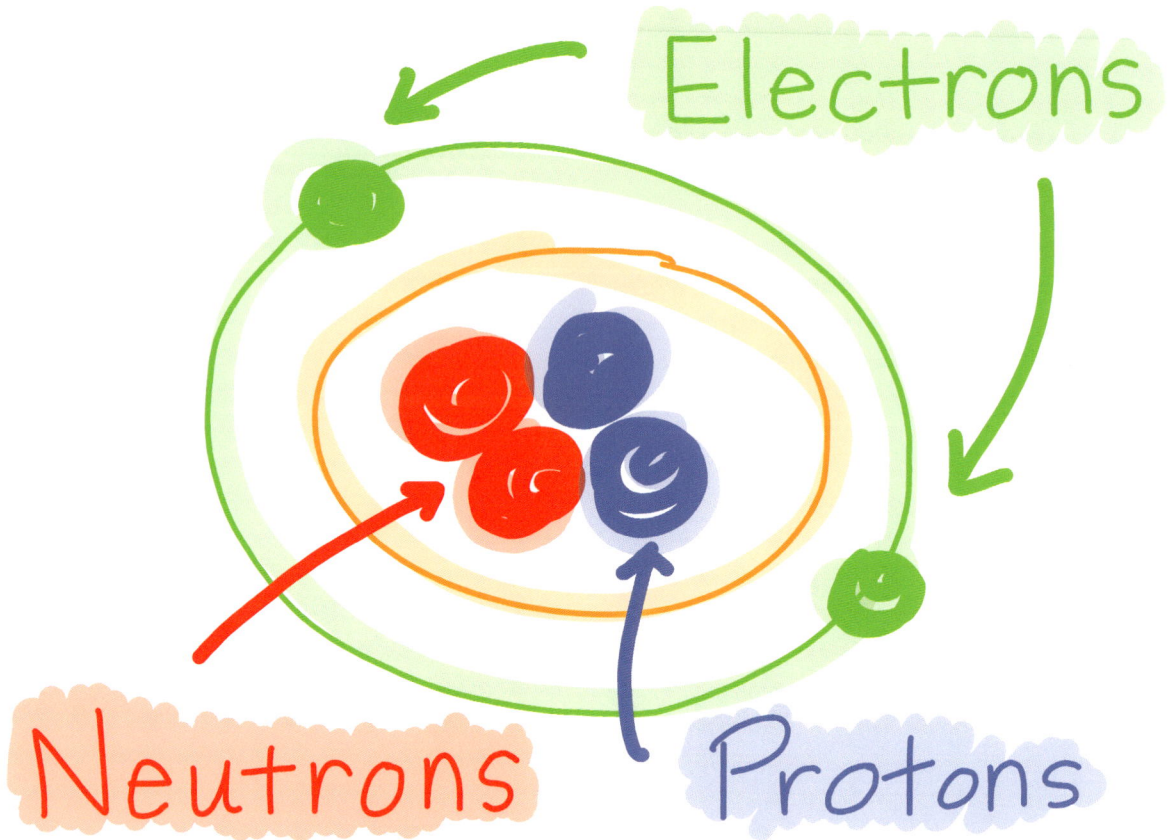

Electrons

Neutrons

Protons

He-li-um

Sound It Out
1. HEE
2. LEE
3. UM

This is an atom of Helium.
The symbol for Helium is He.

Did you see He in the
Periodic Table of Elements?

What is the atomic number
of Helium?

Helium

Helium
makes
balloons
float.

How many electrons
are outside the nucleus
of an atom of Helium?

Carbon

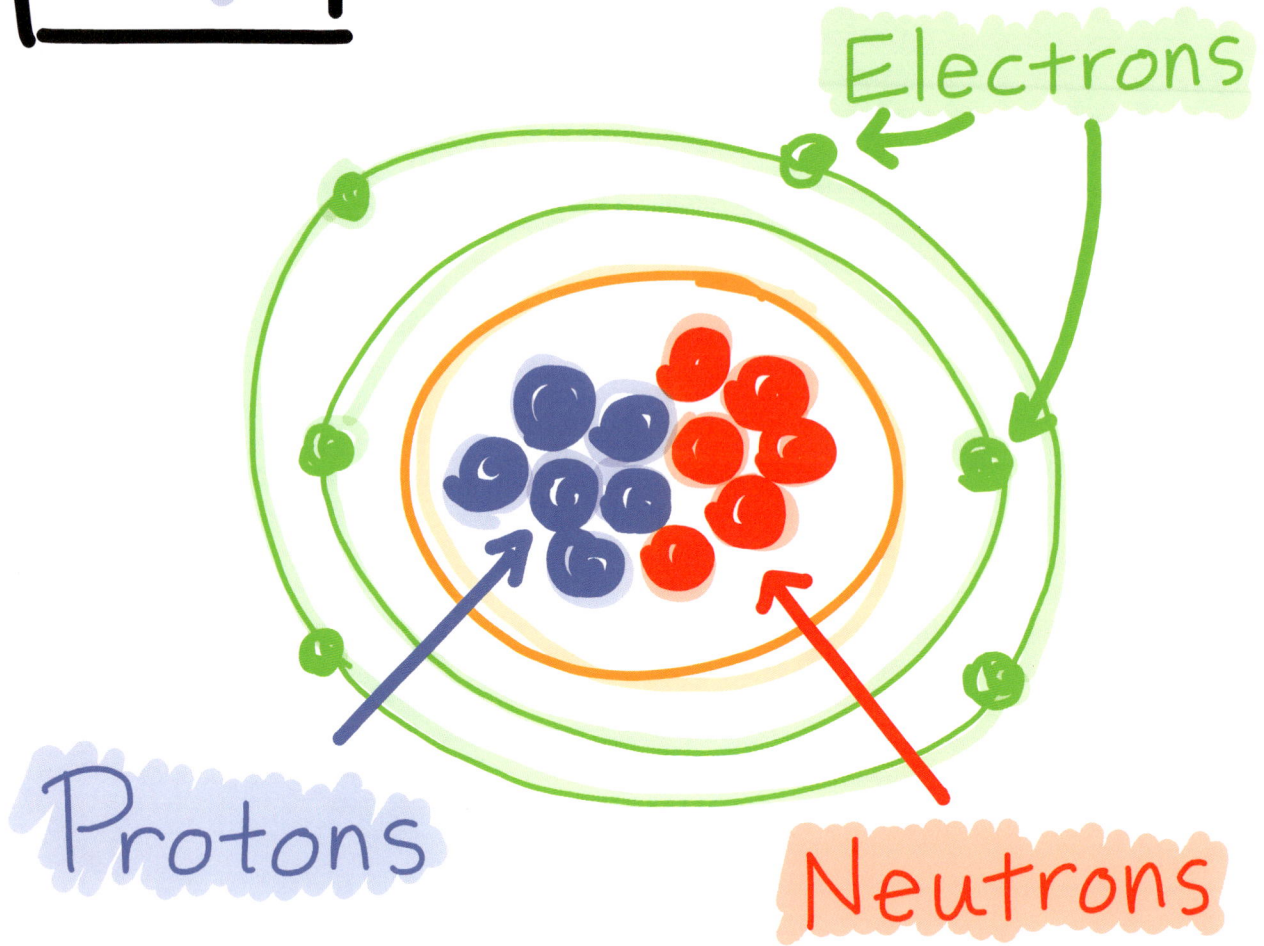

Electrons

Protons

Neutrons

Car-bon

Sound it Out

1. CAR
2. BUN

This is an atom of Carbon.
The symbol for Carbon is C.

Did you see C in the
Periodic Table of Elements?

What is the atomic number
of Carbon?

All living
things are
made of
Carbon.

How many protons
are inside the nucleus
of an atom of Carbon?

You have learned what 3 elements look like as atoms.

Can you name all 3 elements?

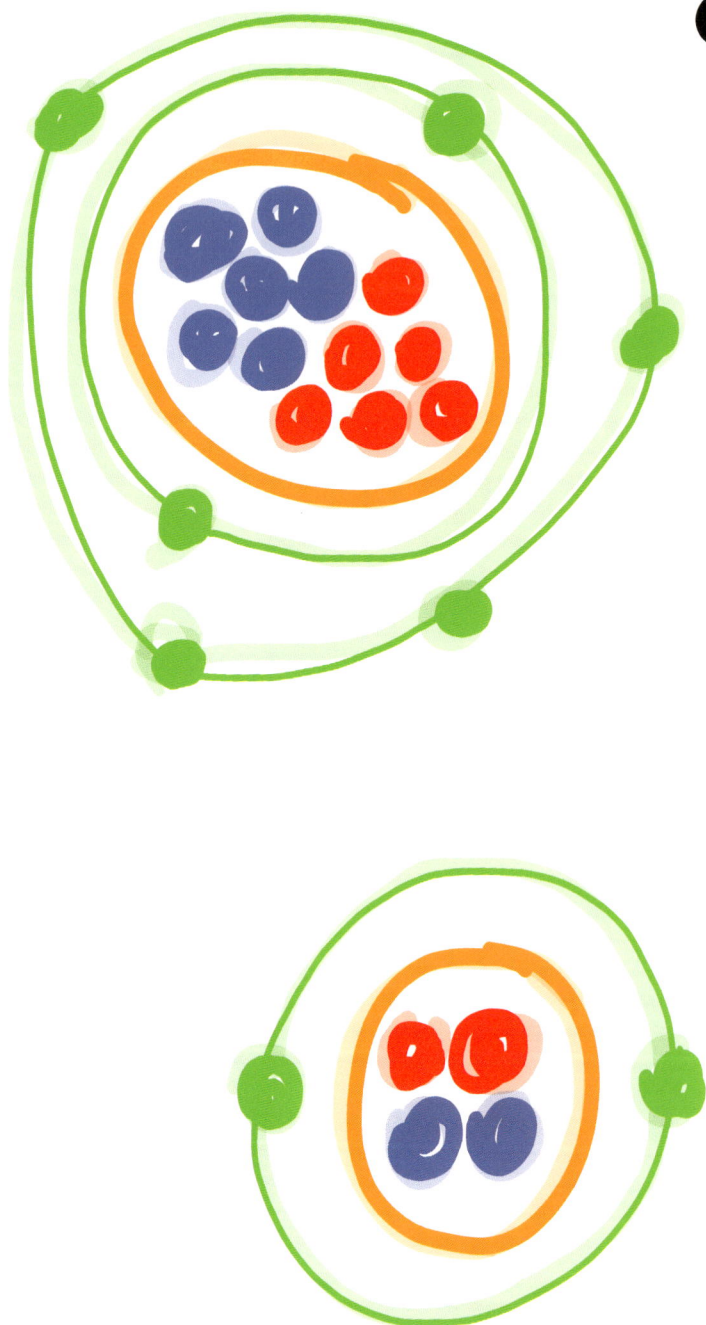

Match the picture with the correct atom.

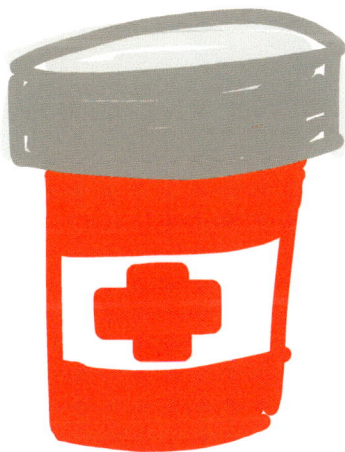

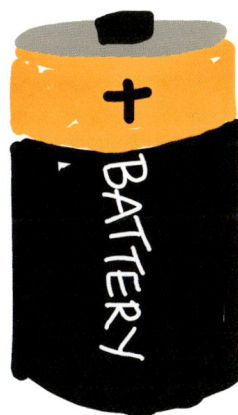

Excellent work! Now we will learn about 3 more elements...

Na

Sodium

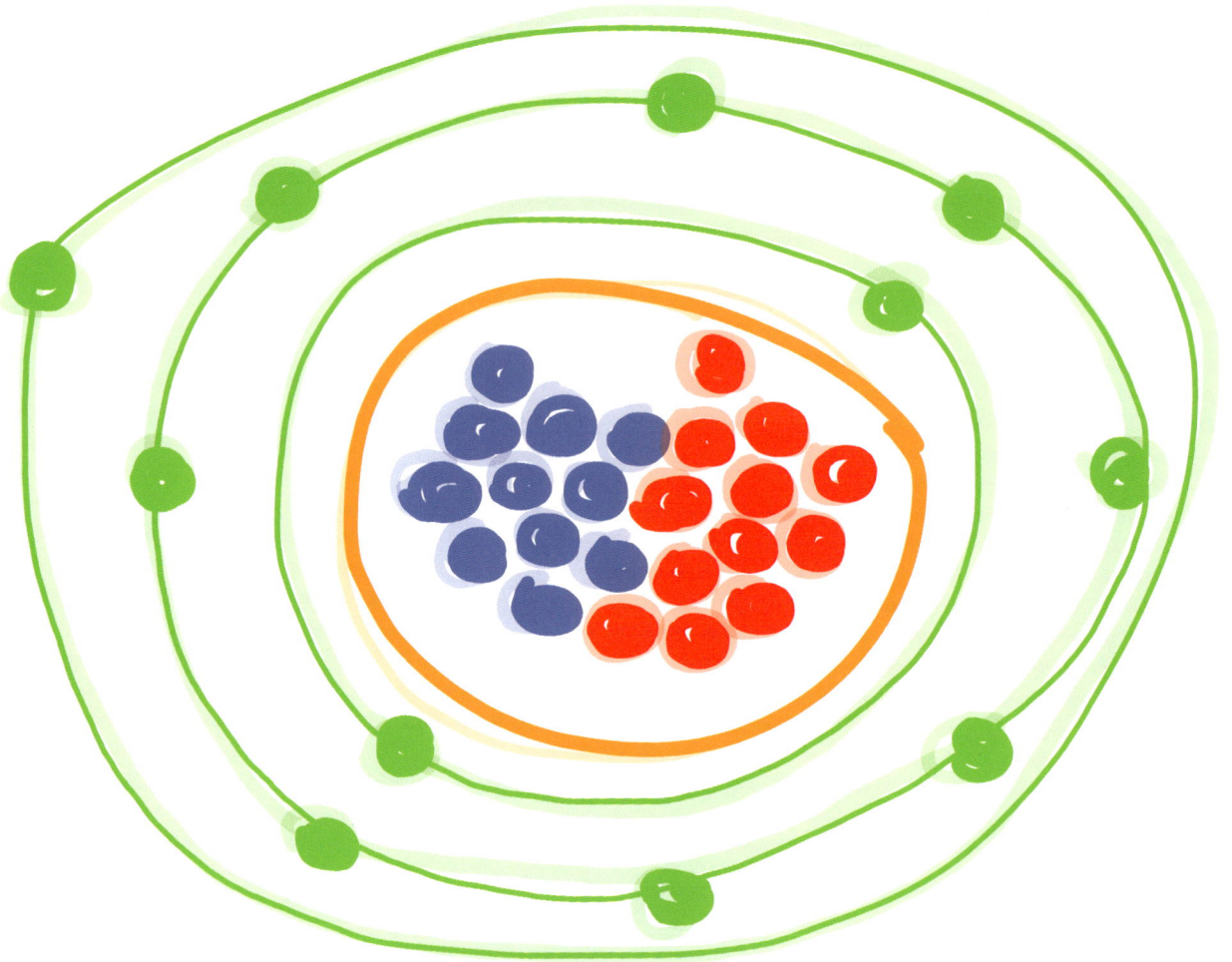

So-di-um

Sound it Out

1. SO
2. DEE
3. UM

This is an atom of Sodium.
The symbol for Sodium is Na.

Did you see Na in the
Periodic Table of Elements?

What is the atomic number
of Sodium?

Sodium
is in
salt.

How many protons
are inside the nucleus
of an atom of Sodium?

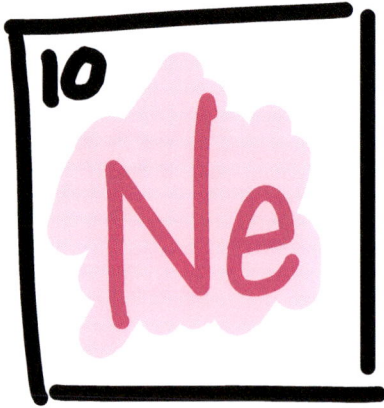

Ne

Neon

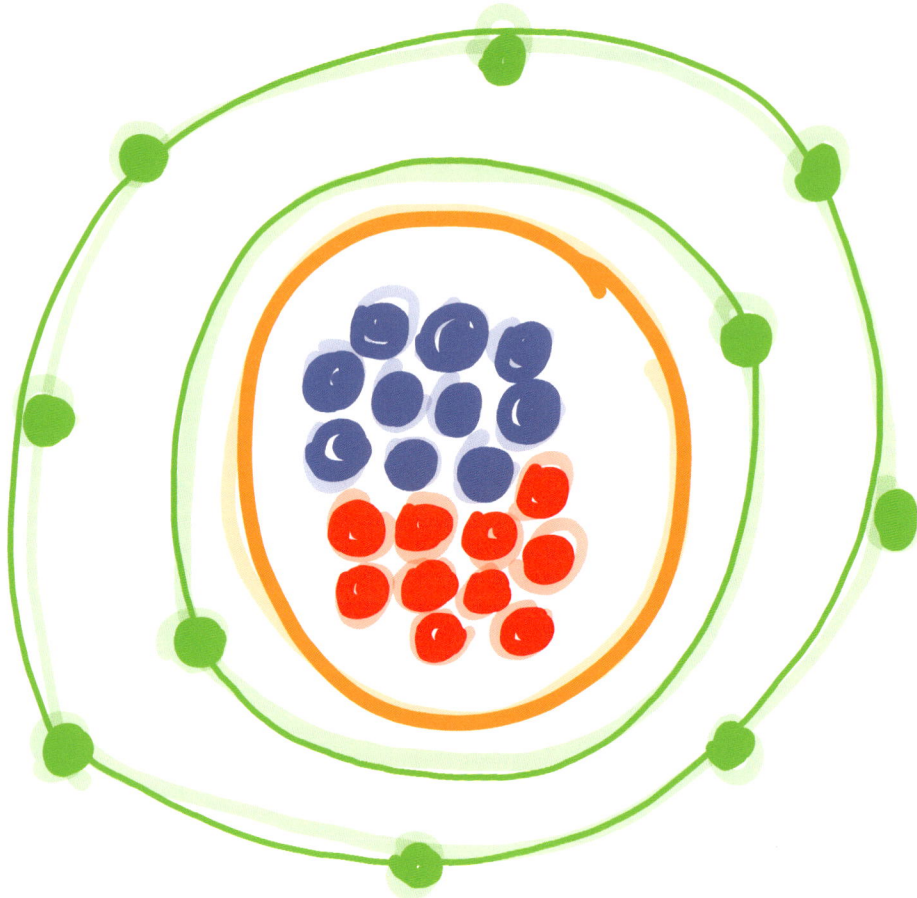

Ne-on

This is an atom of Neon.
The symbol for Neon is Ne.

Did you see Ne in the
Periodic Table of Elements?

What is the atomic number
of Neon?

Neon
is used
to make
signs bright.

OPEN

How many electrons
are outside the nucleus
of an atom of Neon?

O Oxygen

8

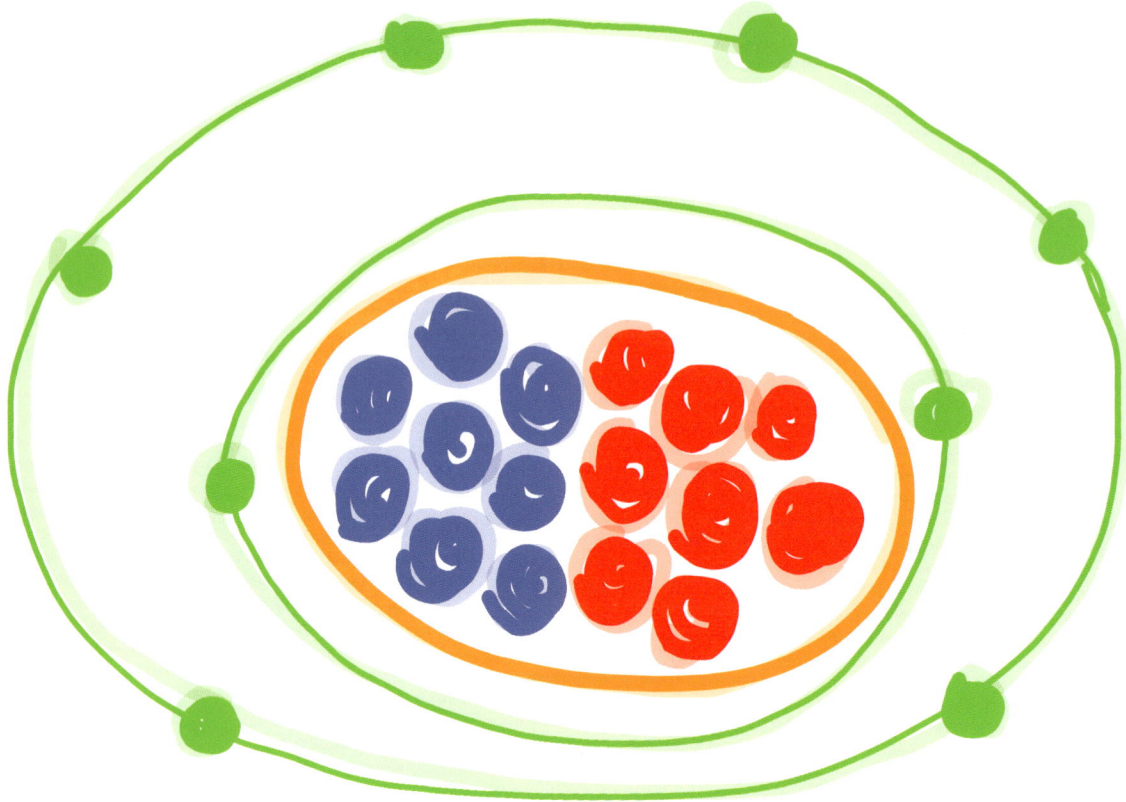

Ox-y-gen

Sound it Out

1. OX
2. EH
3. JEN

This is an atom of Oxygen.
The symbol for Oxygen is O.

Did you see O in the
Periodic Table of Elements?

What is the atomic number
of Oxygen?

Oxygen is in water.

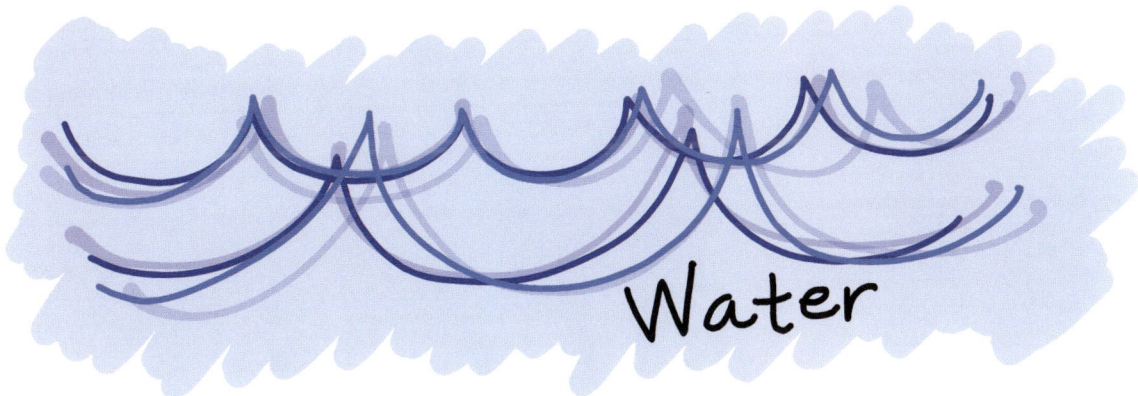

Water

How many protons
are inside the nucleus
of an atom of Oxygen?

You have learned what 3 more elements look like as atoms.

Can you name all 3 elements?

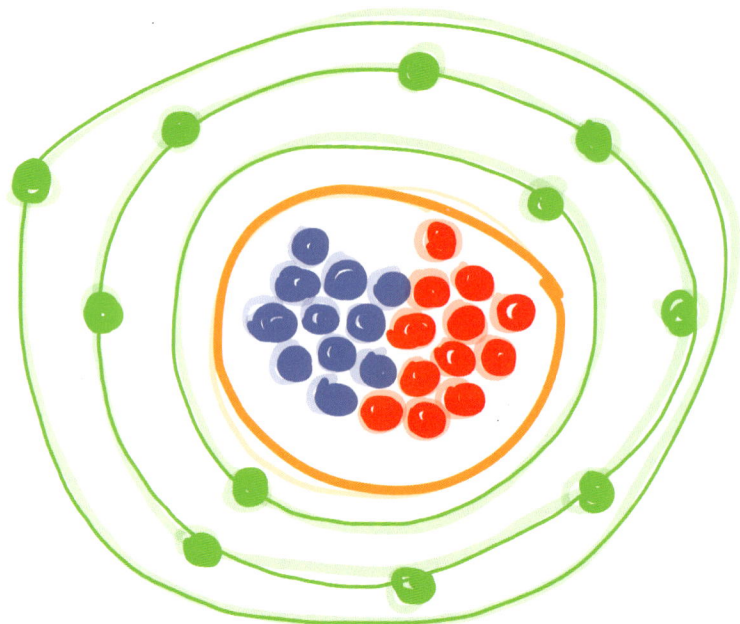

Atomic Number 11

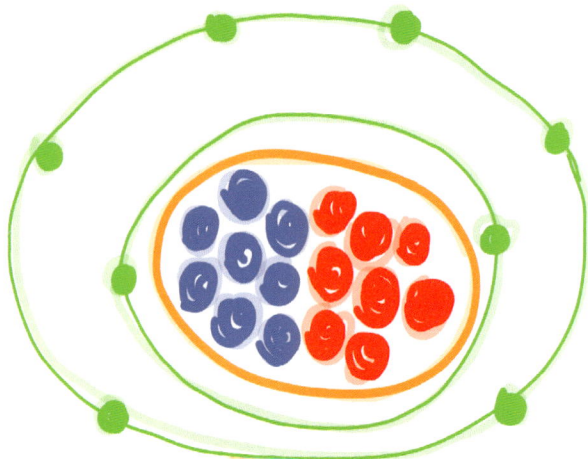

Atomic Number 8

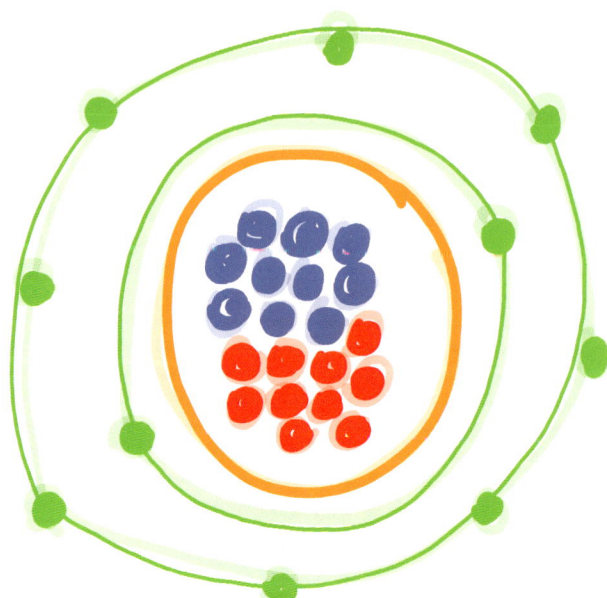

Atomic Number 10

OPEN

Match the picture with the correct atom.

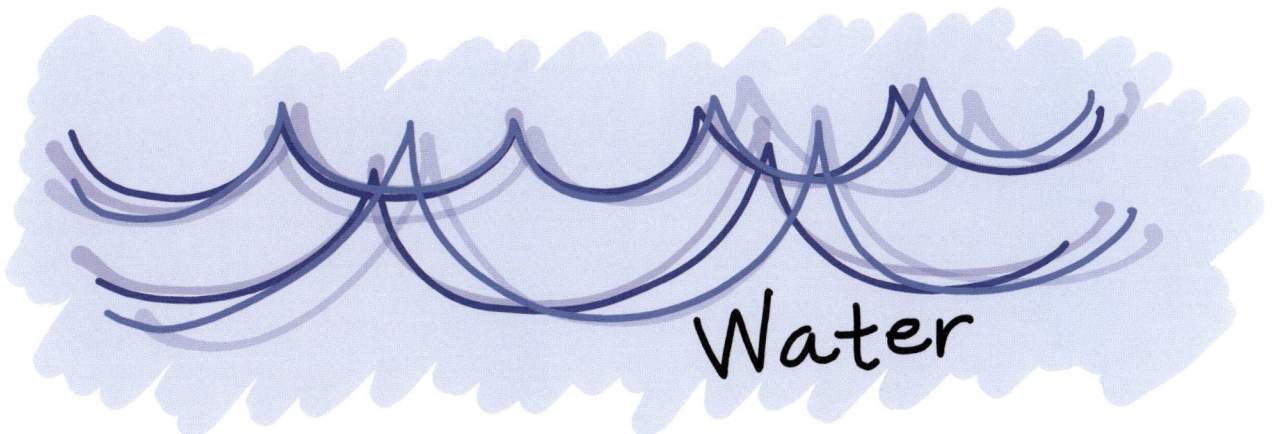

Water

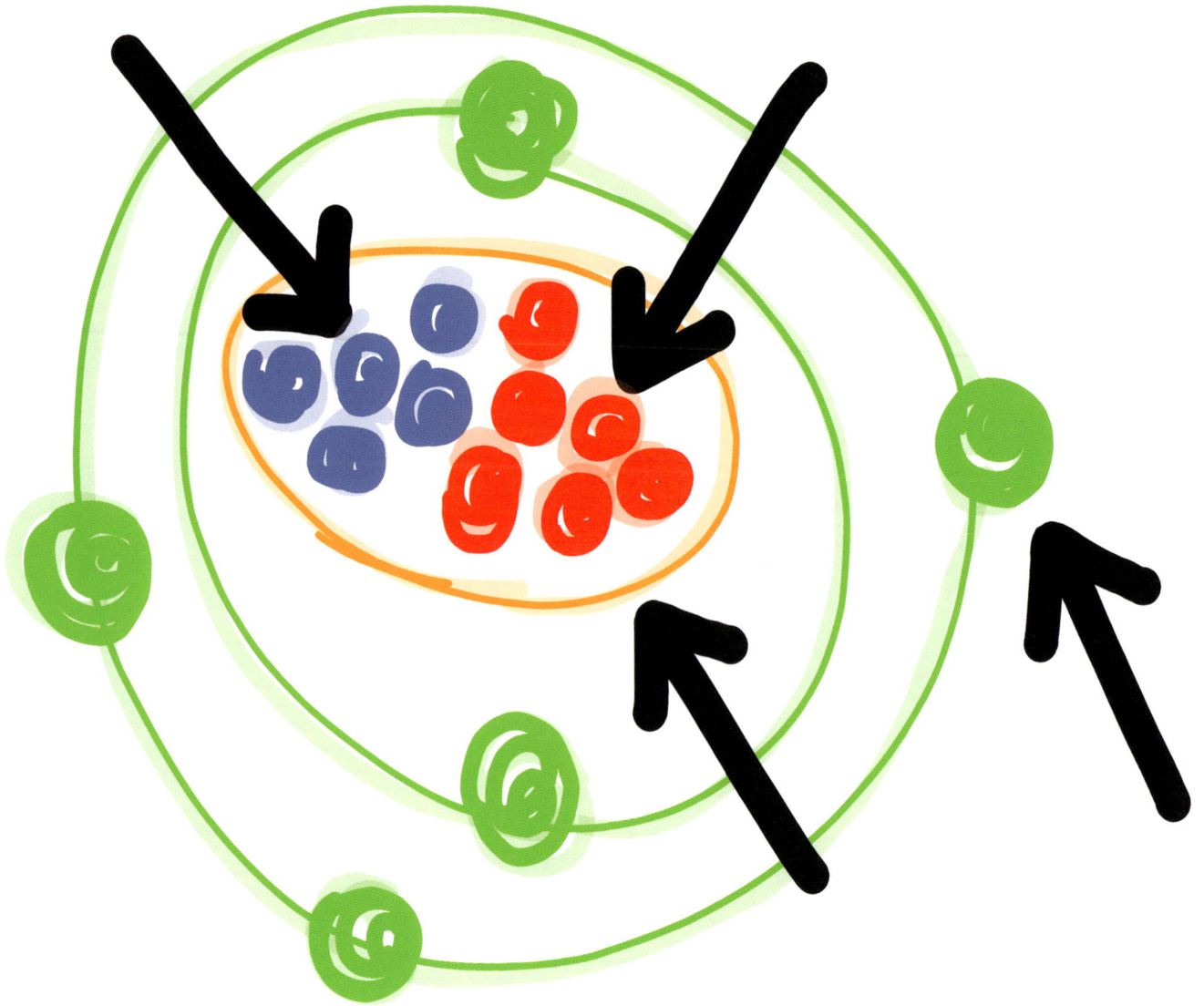

Can you name each
part of this atom?

Practice saying the new words you have learned:

Proton

Neutron

Electron

Atom

Lithium

Helium

Carbon

Nucleus

Element

Sodium

Neon

Oxygen

Atomic Number

Periodic Table of Elements

Great job!

You are a Chemistry expert!

yay science!

Do you have a science topic suggestion for the Super Smart Science Series?
Let us know at www.Facebook.com/SuperSmartScienceSeries.

Submit photos of your family reading our series to be featured on our website!

Free activities and worksheets available online at www.SuperSmartScienceSeries.com.

I have always loved to doodle and draw.
Enjoy these pages and create!

CPSIA information can be obtained
at www.ICGtesting.com
Printed in the USA
LVIC06n1431121113
361025LV00040B/527

* 9 7 8 0 9 8 4 3 8 4 8 5 3 *